The Decorative Stamping Sourcebook

The Decorative Stamping Sourcebook

*200+ designs for making stamps
to decorate your home*

Juliet Bawden

NORTH LIGHT BOOKS

For my father, with lots of love

First published in North America in 1997
by North Light Books
an imprint of F & W Publications, Inc.
1507 Dana Avenue
Cincinnati, OH 45207
1-800/289-0963

First published in Great Britain in 1997
by Collins & Brown Limited, London

1 3 5 7 9 8 6 4 2

Library of Congress Cataloging-in-Publication Data
ISBN 0-89134-790-9

Conceived, edited and designed by Collins & Brown Limited

Editor : Gillian Haslam
Designer: Alison Shackleton
Photography: Shona Wood

Reproduction by Grafiscan, Italy
Printed and bound in Hong Kong by South Sea International

CONTENTS

INTRODUCTION

Welcome to The Decorative Stamping Sourcebook

Stamping is such an easy craft to master that everyone can do it, including young children. However, once you have bought a few stamps you soon discover that you can never find the exact image you are looking for. This is where this book comes in – it is a stamping book with a difference, because as well as providing inspirational photographs of the stamped objects, it also gives you over 200 templates to trace and use for making your own stamps.

Stamping is a very simple and effective way of changing an environment with very little expense. Walls, screens, curtains, chairs, stools, frames, lampshades and stationery boxes are just some of the very many items which were stamped for this book. Lino, foam and sponge can all be used to make stamps. You can also use potatoes and other shaped vegetables and fruits. In fact, we have stamped on an apron with a real apple cut in half.

Stamping is a very easy and creative craft. However, it does take a little practice to perfect. The way in which you apply the paint to the stamp, how much paint you apply and the material from which the stamp is made and the material on which you are stamping will have an effect on the end product. Dense foam, which has a very smooth surface, is best for making intricate stamps. The pattern contained in natural and synthetic sponges shows through as a holey surface on the finished stamp. This can be put to good use on natural shapes such as a starfish or a leaf. Shiny ceramics and tiles are difficult to stamp as the stamp may slide on the surface. In this case it may be worth coating the surface with a matt paint before stamping. There are paints available specifically made for ceramics.

A number of different paints have been used throughout this book including fabric, emulsion and acrylic paints. Many of the acrylic paints are suitable for a variety of surfaces including wood, metal, fabric and walls. It tends to be quick drying and colourfast. It comes in many different finishes – matt, shiny, fluorescent and pearlescent as well as glittery. Read the Materials & Techniques chapter for full instructions before you start.

Stamping may be used to decorate interiors, accessories, presents, the paper in which you wrap the presents and to make the card you send with the present. It is particularly good for festive occasions when you want something special and personalised without having to spend a fortune on something temporary. So, for example, buy some white cotton fabric and stamp it with a chick and egg for an Easter tablecloth or a Christmas tree for the festive season. Or even stamp on a white paper cloth and make napkins to match.

The book is divided into chapters based on themes with lots of ideas to inspire you. You may decide that you like a particular stamp idea but not the way we have used it in the book or the colour we have used. This is where you can reduce or enlarge the image using a photocopier and use it on a different surface using different colours. Sometimes a stamp will look good printed in a row, a circle or a random pattern. Experiment to find out what works best. At the end of each chapter you will find designs for you to trace to make your own stamp.

I hope you enjoy stamping as much as I have while writing this book.

Juliet Bawden

Chapter One

MATERIALS & TECHNIQUES

This chapter includes all the information you need on stamping techniques and materials. I suggest you read it through carefully before you start any of the projects featured in the following chapters. You will soon realise that stamping really is a very simple craft to master, and if you are a beginner, you can start off with a very small amount of inexpensive equipment.

MAKING THE STAMPS

Stamping is a simple and rewarding craft, especially for those who like quick results.
However, after using lots of shop-bought stamps the images can begin to pall. It is so much
more rewarding and fun to create your own images. It is very easy as stamps can be made
from many different materials including cork, wood, lino or vegetables.

CUTTING A STAMP FROM A POTATO

Vegetables like potatoes have been used as stamps for many years. They are very simple to use – simply slice and carve out the motifs, wipe to remove moisture and apply the paint. As well as potatoes, you can use anything from peppers to apples and pears.

You will need

A FIRM POTATO

MARKER PEN

SHARP KNIFE WITH AN
UNSERRATED BLADE

CHOPPING BOARD

KITCHEN PAPER

CRAFT KNIFE

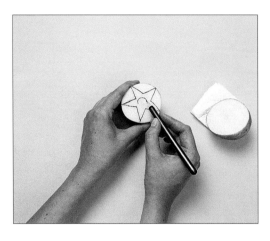

1 *Place the potato on the chopping board and cut it in half with the sharp knife. Do this in one smooth motion so that the surface is straight. Draw your motif directly onto the potato with the pen. It is best to keep the motif very simple.*

2 *Take the craft knife and carefully score out the excess potato. Make one cut at an angle and make the next cut at an angle to that so they meet in a V, remove the background. Stamp the potato on the kitchen towel to dry off the moisture.*

STAMP MAKING TIP

A potato stamp will only last for a few hours, so begin to stamp immediately. If you keep a copy of the design, you can then use a fresh potato if you need to.

CUTTING A STAMP FROM SPONGE

Sponge is a great material for making stamps as the textures of each stamp vary according to the density of the sponge. The denser the sponge, the more definite and precise the outline of the stamped image will be; the looser the sponge, the more indefinite the outline. The amount of paint the sponge soaks up can also affect the final image. Play around with sponge stamps as the variations of effects are enormous.

Sponge stamps can be used on all stampable surfaces. As soon as you have finished stamping with your sponge, run it under warm water and squeeze it, until the water runs clear.

You will need

TRACING PAPER

PAPER

PENCIL

FINE MARKER PEN

SCISSORS

SPONGE

1 *Trace a template from one of the sections in this book. Draw over the traced line on the back of the tracing paper. Trace the image onto white paper.*

2 *Carefully cut out the paper template following the traced outline.*

3 *Using the fine marker pen, draw around the template onto the sponge.*

4 *Using scissors, cut out the sponge stamp and neaten any rough edges.*

CUTTING A STAMP FROM FOAM BOARD

Foam board is good for a motif with many different, disconnected elements, for example a flower with many separate petals. The top layer of paper and the central layer of foam can be removed, while the lower, thicker layer of paper holds the parts of the stamp together. It is also good for designs with fine lines.

The disadvantage of this board is that after a while the paper tends to become soggy and peel away, so use your stamp swiftly and discard it if it becomes unusable. Keep your template to re-make the stamp if necessary.

A foam board stamp works really well on walls, wood and fabric. Avoid using it on glass and ceramics as the stamp will slide too easily.

You will need

FOAM BOARD

TRACING PAPER

PENCIL

CRAFT KNIFE

CARBON PAPER

SELF-HEALING
CUTTING MAT

1 *Choose a design from the templates provided. Trace over the image onto tracing paper.*

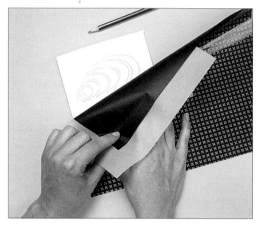

2 *Place the tracing paper on top of a piece of carbon paper and place the carbon ink side down on the foam board. Draw heavily on top of the lines of the design to transfer it through the carbon onto the board.*

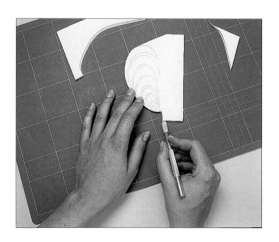

3 *Using a pencil, go over the outline to add any missed parts. The image can now be seen clearly, making it easier to follow the outline when cutting out. Use a very sharp craft knife to cut the outer shape of the image.*

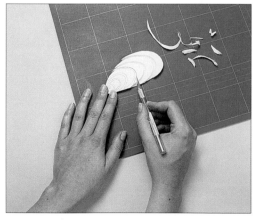

4 *Taking care to cut away only the top layer of card and the central layer of foam, cut out the pattern from the centre of the design. The bottom layer of card will prevent it falling apart. You are now ready to start stamping.*

CUTTING A STAMP FROM FOAM SHEET

Foam sheeting is the best stamping material I have come across. It is thin, pliable, easy to cut and transfers paint well. Stamps made from this are ideal for most surfaces, including paper, wood, walls, glass, ceramics and fabric. It is the easiest material to use on rounded surfaces because it is so pliable.

Because foam sheeting is quite thin, it is probably a good idea to attach it to a handle as you may have problems lifting the stamp off the surface. Glue the stamp onto a transparent plastic lid so you see exactly where you are stamping. Because the foam sheet has an identical surface on the back, it is possible to flip the stamp over and use the reverse as a mirror image.

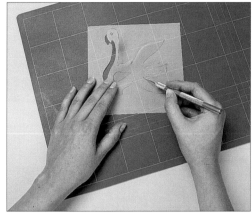

You will need

5MM (¼ IN) THICK FOAM SHEET

TRACING PAPER

FINE MARKER PEN

PENCIL

SHARP CRAFT KNIFE

SELF-HEALING CUTTING MAT

1 *Trace off your chosen motif by placing the tracing paper over the image. Holding the paper firmly, trace around the edges of the motif carefully with a sharp pencil.*

2 *Place the tracing paper with the image drawn on it on the cutting mat. Slowly and steadily cut out the image with the craft knife. Hold the knife as you would a pencil.*

3 *Lay the paper image down on the foam sheet. Holding it securely in place, use this as a template and carefully draw around its edges with a dark marker pen. Remove the template to reveal the outline of the motif on the foam sheet.*

4 *Take the sharp craft knife and very carefully cut along the marker line. Keep your hand steady and cut in one smooth stroke, as stopping makes the cut jagged. For safety, always cut away from yourself in case the knife slips.*

13

CUTTING A STAMP FROM LINO

Lino is a traditional printing material and many of us used this in art class while still at school. It is quite a soft material which can be carved without difficulty. A lino cutting kit will provide all the tools required. When carving lino, always carve away from yourself, pushing the lino tool and scooping the excess lino out.

Lino is ideal for printing large areas, especially fabrics and paper. It is also suitable for making detailed stamps. Use a lino roller to apply paint and a heavy roller to apply pressure on the back of the piece so that the paint is transferred evenly. Wipe lino clean with a damp cloth; do not get lino wet as it will curl up.

You will need

LINO

LINO CUTTING TOOL

SHARP CRAFT KNIFE

TRACING PAPER

CARBON PAPER

SHARP PENCIL

SELF-HEALING CUTTING MAT

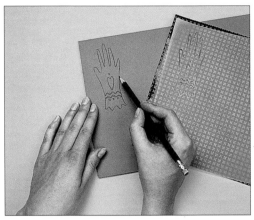

1 *Place the tracing paper on the image and trace it off. Lay the lino smooth side up, then place the carbon paper, carbon side down on the lino and place the tracing over that. Reverse the traced image so that when cut out, it will be identical to the template.*

2 *Draw heavily over the traced outline, so that the image will transfer through the carbon paper onto the lino. When you remove the tracing and carbon paper, the image should be clear. If not, touch it up with the pencil, copying the template.*

3 *Place the lino on the mat and cut around the outline with the craft knife. With the no. 1 lino cutting tool, score along the marked lines. Push the blade into the lino and away from yourself. The blade will pick up the lino and score into the surface.*

4 *If you have larger areas of lino to remove, change the blade to a no. 2 or 3 and score the lino out, making sure you push the lino tool away from your body. It is the lino that remains which will make the decorative impression when stamped.*

USEFUL EQUIPMENT

As you will see, very little specialised equipment is required for stamping. You will probably already have some of the tools listed below, and others can be bought at good craft shops.

Tracing paper

Use tracing paper to trace off the templates in this book and to trace images from other books, pictures and magazines. Grided tracing paper is good if you want to enlarge images. Tracing paper motifs can also be cut out and used as templates to draw around on the foam sheeting.

Carbon paper

Carbon paper can be used sandwiched between your traced images and the surface of your stamping material, with the carbon side down. This is ideal to duplicate your chosen motif onto lino or foam board. However, it does not work on foam sheeting.

Fine marker pen and pencil

Use a fine black marker pen to draw around your templates onto foam sheeting. A pencil is needed for tracing and sketching.

Craft knife and scissors

A good, sharp craft knife with extra blades is necessary when cutting out templates and stamps. If the blade is not sharp enough, the edge of your stamp will be jagged and rough when cut, so change the blade as soon as it starts to become blunt. Use scissors for cuttings things out roughly, before starting to cut out the detail.

Lino cutter and tools

A lino cutter is needed when cutting lino and scoring out the design. There are usually five tools in a lino cutting kit, ranging from number one which is the thinnest and sharpest (this is used for making the first scores) up to number five which is the widest (used for scooping out the excess lino).

Self-healing cutting mat

When using a craft knife, work on a suitable surface. For this purpose, a self-healing cutting mat is ideal. An alternative to this is a small sheet of glass.

Paint brushes

A selection of paint brushes in various sizes is useful for priming surfaces, painting backgrounds, applying paint to stamps, touching up, adding detail and, finally, varnishing.

Sponge roller

A sponge roller is the best way to apply paint to a stamp. It absorbs paint evenly and when rolled onto the stamp, it distributes paint smoothly across it so that when the stamp is used, no paint marks are visible, as when a paint brush is used.

Lino roller

A lino roller is used particularly for applying colour to a piece of lino. It is similar to the sponge roller, except that it is made from solid rubber. This means that the paint is not absorbed by the roller, but is pushed and spread smoothly around the lino surface.

STAMPING TIP

Keep your tools in good condition by washing them after use and storing them in a dry place.

WHICH PAINTS FOR WHICH SURFACES?

For the best results, it is important that you choose the correct type of paint for the surface you wish to stamp on. If you are a beginner, always practise your design on a piece of scrap paper first.

Fabrics

Fabric paints are a great invention. However, you can only stamp dark colours on light fabrics, and not light on dark because the paint soaks into the fabric. Alternatively, you can use certain acrylic paints which are suitable for fabric and sit on the surface of the fabric, so you can stamp a lighter colour onto a dark fabric. The outlines are also a lot sharper with this paint.

When using acrylic paints on fabrics, you must first read the manufacturer's instructions. Ironing on the reverse side of the fabric fixes certain types of acrylic paint and makes it colourfast. If you are going to stamp on a fabric with shrinkage, wash the fabric and iron it flat before stamping.

Wood

If you wish to stamp on untreated wood, first sand the surface slightly to remove any roughness. If you prefer to paint the surface, there are numerous ways to prepare the wood. With untreated wood, a quick and effective paint job is a wash in diluted acrylic or emulsion paint. Apply watered down paint with a thick brush and then rub the paint into the grain with an old rag until the grain is noticeable. Painted surfaces should also be sanded first.

If you wish to paint the wood a strong colour, always prime the surface first in white. Gesso is generally recommended for priming, but in most cases, white emulsion will suffice. Then paint your background colour with acrylic or emulsion paint. Apply two or three coats. This will give a smooth and even finish.

Stamp your motifs using the same types of emulsion or acrylic paints. When the motifs are dry, protect the stamps with a coat of matt polyurethane varnish.

Paper

Paper and card are the easiest surfaces on which to stamp. All types of paint can be used and every kind of stamp is suitable for use on these surfaces.

Glass and ceramics

When working on ceramics, choose rough china and avoid objects with a highly glossy finish as they are extremely difficult to stamp on. Sand surfaces first with the finest sandpaper to give the surface a texture to which the paint can adhere.

Use ceramic paint when stamping on china. This has a thick and slippery texture, very different to water-based paints, and the slippery paint and smooth surface can cause the stamp to slide around. When you lift the stamp, the transferred image can be messy. If necessary, touch up the image with a fine brush.

When stamping on glass, use ceramic paints as glass paints are transparent. Use small, simple stamps so there is less chance of making mistakes.

It is best to stamp on ceramics to be used purely for decorative purposes or check that the paint is suitable for contact with food or drinks.

STAMPING TIP

When buying cans of emulsion paint, select the small sample ones. This means you can build up a large collection of varied colours without having to store the full-size cans.

APPLYING PAINT

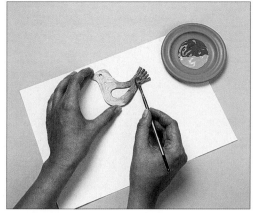

1 *The most even way to apply paint is with a small sponge roller. Pour a small amount of paint onto a flat plate and push the roller over the paint, until it is evenly covered. Carefully roll the paint over the stamp. When stamping with lino, use a rubber lino roller to achieve the correct effect.*

2 *A brush is the most common way of applying paint, allowing you to control the amount of paint. You can brush different colours onto the same stamp to create varied effects. Brush marks are visible once you have stamped, especially on fabric. If you do not like this, touch it up with a fine paint brush.*

STAMPING TIP

If you are stamping with a sponge, pour the paint onto a flat plate and spread it out into an thin even layer and then dip. Always ensure that the sponge has an even coat of paint.

MAKING A PAINT PAD

An alternative method is to use a paint pad. This is used by simply pressing the stamp firmly onto the pad until it is covered with paint. You can buy ink pads especially for stamping or you can make your own. The ideal container is a plastic tub with a lid, so that the paint doesn't dry out.

You will need

PLASTIC CONTAINER WITH A LID, *e.g. A* MARGARINE TUB

DOMESTIC SPONGE

MUSLIN OR THIN COTTON FABRIC

SCISSORS

SPOON

PAINT

1 *Wash out the plastic container thoroughly. Using scissors, cut the sponge so that it fits snugly into the container. Wrap the sponge in the muslin or cotton fabric and place it into the container.*

2 *Dilute the paint with water and pour it directly onto the covered sponge. Spread and firmly press the paint evenly around the sponge pad with a spoon until it has been thoroughly absorbed.*

Chapter Two

CLASSIC LIVING

The simplicity and elegance of ancient and classical architecture have inspired decorative features from the times of the ancient Greeks and Romans. There are many popular motifs that are, in essence, Romanesque or Greek, from silhouettes of jugs and vases to laurel wreaths, facial profiles and swags of material.

The clean lines and elegant shapes of Greek columns, stone urns and swirling wall carvings have inspired the following stamps featured here.

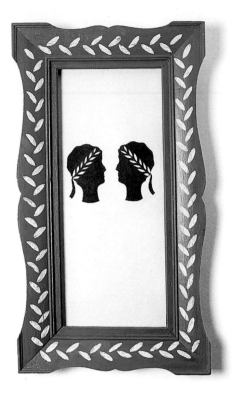

The smooth lines and classic shapes of these designs make drawing and cutting stamps relatively easy. If you want to use sources other than this book to create classic stamps, simply use tracing paper to copy the design you see and then simplify it to a form that is suitable for a stamp. If an image is symmetrical, copy one exact half of the image and then fold the tracing paper in half and trace over the drawn half. When you unfold the paper the image should be identical on both sides. If you are cutting symmetrical shapes, make sure you cut them out accurately, as they can look lopsided once you have stamped a few, especially if you are stamping them in a row or in a systematic pattern.

Creating a theme

Architectural details from the Roman and Greek buildings are good source materials for stamping designs, in that they are quite simple shapes and can be transferred into stamps with very little alteration to the original motif. The leaves from a laurel may be stamped in a traditional wreath pattern or used to decorate the edge of a frame. Here the frame is painted in a classic shade of deep green with white stamps.

The silhouette of an urn or jug is a solid shape which can be traced and cut without difficulty. The more intricate patterns taken from engravings and mouldings can be transferred into stamps by taking a single repeating shape from the pattern and using it to create a similar repeat pattern for a border or suchlike. In fact, try taking two or three elements out of a complicated design, create stamps from them and stamp them individually or in formation to produce interesting results.

Laurel leaf frame

A junk shop find has been given a lick of green paint, and then a simple leaf shape, cut from an eraser, has been stamped all around the edge to create a simple white laurel border.

Cotton-edged towels

Strips of cotton were stamped with a mixture of silver and black fabric paint, to produce a pewter shade. They were then hand sewn onto the towel borders as a decorative edge. The Greek key and wave patterns are instantly recognisable classical motifs.

The rituals of bathing seem to be a long forgotten pleasure, until you begin to research the visual art of our ancient ancestors. Take a look at the wall reliefs of people bathing, washing each other and pouring urns of water. The images of bathers could easily be used as stamp designs for a bathroom or a dressing room. By using mosaic-like patterns or cube shapes to stamp on tiles surrounding your wash basin or bath tub, you can create simple and crisp patterns that are reminiscent of Roman baths. Continue the theme by stamping laurel borders on towels and face cloths and pile them up beside the bath. Decorate accessories like soap dishes, toothbrush holders and cabinets with details taken from mouldings and reliefs, to tie in with the classic theme.

If you are stamping an entire room and its furnishings in a certain theme, it is probably better to stamp just borders and details on each object rather than saturate the room with too many images. So be careful when planning what and where you are going to stamp in order to avoid an over-busy look.

Mosaic-style tiles

Grey linoleum tiles have been stamped using a small sponge cube dipped in silver and black paint. The stamps are placed close together in rows to achieve a 'mosaic' or cobbled pattern.

The mosaic look

Roman architects recognised that if a floor was particularly decorative, it would give an exceptionally luxurious feel to the surroundings, so many floors consisted of decorated or coloured and shaped tiles and elaborate mosaics. Here, to replicate this look, a bathroom floor has been cleverly disguised by stamping, using silver and black floor paint onto simple adhesive-backed floor tiles. A look of authenticity is achieved by applying different amounts of pressure when stamping the tiles. The stamp is a cube cut from a domestic sponge, which has been dipped in paint and then stamped in rows along the tile, close to each other, so that it looks like small tiles laid close together.

Skirtings, friezes and doors can be stamped with the same or complimentary designs used at a smaller scale. This is an ideal way to link stamped accessories to the main decor of the room.

The steel grey and silver theme has been used here to create the classic bathroom shown in the main photograph. Bursts of colour are added with brightly coloured soaps and pink flowers. Butter muslin curtains have been stamped with a stylised wave pattern using silver fabric paint. When working on something as fine and loosely woven as butter muslin, place an absorbent fabric beneath the muslin to take up any excess paint. To complete the look, the pelmet has a shadow swirl pattern.

To embellish plain towels, as shown on page 20, stamp onto preshrunk plain cotton fabric using fabric paint. The stamps used in this bathroom were a classical jug, Greek key and the shadow swirl pattern, as on the pelmet. After the fabric had been stamped, it was ironed on the back to fix the design and then sewn onto white towels as a border.

Changing the colour scheme

Depending on the colours used, the effects achieved can be quite different from one another. Classic monochromes of black, white and grey give a crisp and classic touch, whereas bronzes and golds create a more opulent Baroque feel. Border patterns with classical influences used in primary colour schemes can give a room a more contemporary feel.

Muslin curtains

Silver shadow swirls were stamped on butter muslin curtains with silver fabric paint which stands out in relief on the fine fabric; the motif echoes the fold and sway of the fine fabric.

The fleur de lys is one of those timeless motifs which is constantly popular. It has been used to very good effect here to pull together a lamp, its base and a wooden platter. The lamp base and the platter were both given a base coat of black acrylic paint and then rubbed with gold highlighting wax. The fleur de lys was stamped on the shade using a gold acrylic paint suitable for both absorbent and non-absorbent surfaces. The stamp used was made from high density foam.

Depending on the material of the actual stamp the finished effect can vary. For example, if the stamp is cut from a solid substance like high density foam or rubber, the stamped image will be clear and crisp and identical to the actual stamp. However, if the stamp is cut from sponge or lino, the stamped image will be textured and will probably result in an uneven image. However, this is one of the beauties of stamping, in that an uneven, slightly ragged image can be just as interesting and effective as a perfectly formed image.

Fleur de lys lampshade
The fleur de lys is an ever-popular classical motif. In this instance it has been stamped in gold acrylic paint around the lower edge of a plain black fabric lampshade.

23

Templates

The most obvious of classical Roman and Grecian inspired motifs are the ever-present urns and vessels These are perfect stamps for the bathroom – stamp them in silvers and greys for a cool effect or in golds and coppers for a more opulent Baroque look.

The laurel leaf can be cut as a row of leaves to make a border pattern. Alternatively a single stamp can be cut and then each time it is stamped they can be placed close together to create a laurel border.

Cut the mosaic square from lino and stamp it using ceramic paint onto tiles or, even simpler, cut a cube of sponge and stamp the cube onto a tile in rows, very close to each other to give them a pebbled look.

The fleur de lys, profile and Greek key are all classic shapes that can be stamped in all manner of colours and sizes and still be recognised for their classic theme.

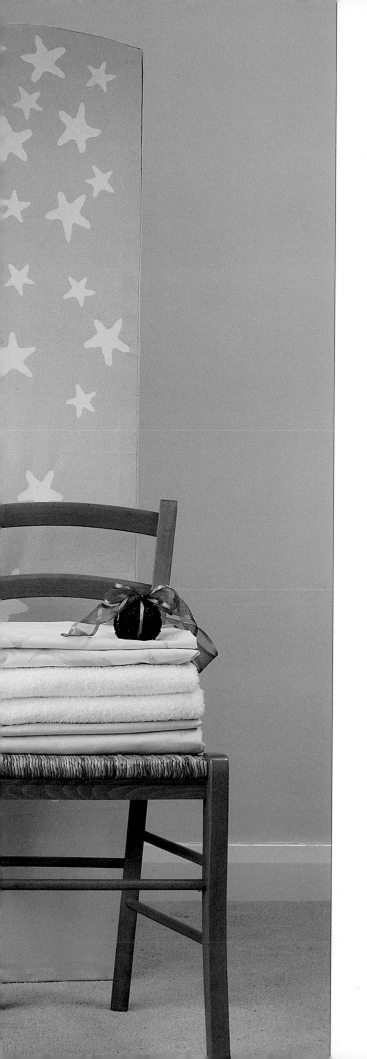

Chapter Three

MARINE WORLD

Over 70 per cent of our planet is covered in water supporting a huge variety of plant and marine life which provides good reference for designers. Shells, fish, starfish, sea birds, seaweed and waves can all be translated into patterns for stamping. Here an old junk shop screen was re-covered with artists' canvas and the edges covered in bias binding. Three starfish stamps cut from a domestic sponge, each one smaller than the other, have been stamped onto the screen using white acrylic paint.

We automatically think of bathrooms when stamping such watery images, but they can also look great on china, bed linen and fabric and in other settings as well as the bathroom. For example, a recessed window can be given focus by framing it with a stamped pattern of stylised waves curling around fish who appear to dart between the waves.

A curling tendril of seaweed can hold many different stamped images together, such as on a frieze. Between the seaweed stamp shells, fish, starfish and crabs in soft ice cream colours. Or use neutral tones of stone, parchment, cream and magnolia for a more sophisticated version of the same image.

We automatically think of anything to do with the sea as being blue or green but the movement of water makes for many subtle colour changes. There are endless colours and many kinds of paints which can be used to reflect this movement. For example, try pearlised paints developed for use on fabrics or glass paints which are transparent to give a wonderful watery feel. By stamping a soft colour and then the same stamp in a more defined colour you can create a feeling of movement.

Revamping a bathroom

Whatever material they are made from, stamps rarely give a flat, even surface. This can be used to good effect when stamping shells, which naturally look hard-edged in some places and sea-smoothed in others. These stamps look very pretty round a plain, broad-fronted picture or mirror frame. Tired looking bathroom cabinets can benefit from a coat of paint and a stamped design of fish. For an etched style mirror, mix white emulsion or stamping paint with a small amount of ready mixed

Fish lampshade

A plain parchment-coloured lampshade has been stamped with a simple fish motif to create a lively design. The same stamp was used to decorate the hessian-covered photograph album, showing the range and versatility of this technique.

Bathroom tiles

An ordinary white ceramic tile splashback above a hand basin has been livened up with bright orange and yellow starfish stamps. The contrasting dots were added with a paintbrush.

wallpaper paste and dip a fish stamp made from dense sponge into it. Stamp onto the mirror and leave to dry. The result will be a soft white fish. If the image is not sufficiently strong, simply wash it off and start again using less paste and more paint.

Waves have been used in many different cultures as decoration, including Roman mosaics, Chinese embroidery, American patchwork quilts and Japanese paper cuts. They can be a simple curl, something with a scalloped undercurrent or even with an over-stamp of bubbles. They look good stamped onto tiles or on a bathroom wall. What a treat to lie in the bath and look at the waves, imagining you are somewhere far more exotic.

For less natural, more man-made imagery of the sea, there are nautical elements such as anchors, life belts and ropes. Ropes make lovely stamps if you have a long thin area to decorate. Break up the space with a stamped rope, making it horizontal, vertical or looped depending on the illusion you are trying to create and the available space.

Wooden shell box
Sea shells are a popular bathroom design. Here a pretty shell motif has been stamped in gold to give a plain wash bag a stylish border. The blue colourwashed box has been decorated with an attractive mussel shell motif in white, while the plain white tiles have been stamped with a whelk shell motif.

Padded storage boxes

*A shoe box has been covered in calico,
the lid was lined with wadding before
it was covered to give it some padding.
Once covered, a small shell stamp was
stamped randomly all over it in a dense
coffee brown colour, to complement the
soft colours in this dressing room set.*

The same image can be used in a number of ways on different surfaces,
for example, an elegant fish may look as lovely round a lampshade as on
a photo album. On the example shown here, the stamp was made from
thin dense foam which is very pliable. This allowed the fish to be moved
to create different shaped fish. A similar fish cut slightly larger in scale is
stamped onto pure white pillowcases using parchment pigment.

Starfish and shells

Sea shells come in many different shapes and sizes and can look very
realistic when stamped together. Because they are often segmented, the
design can be exaggerated to give a stylised image of a shell. For example
in the mussel shell box shown on page 33, the areas that are usually

ridges in a real shell have been cut out to make a defined pattern.

Keeping to the same colour palette with white, parchment, cream, rust and off-white, a dressing room can be created around an old screen. This was stripped of its old leatherette fabric and re-covered in natural looking canvas. It was then stamped with starfishes cut from sponge. These ranged in size and were placed randomly all over the screen. A natural calico wash stand has been stamped in white along one edge with a simple wave pattern. Shoe boxes have been given a coat of white emulsion to rid them of any print which may show through the stamped calico. They were then covered in calico and stamped with a shell design. The lids have had a piece of thin wadding placed under the calico to give them some body.

The sea theme is taken back to a bathroom setting, this time with another image of starfish used very differently to decorate some rather ordinary tiles round a basin. Bright yellow and orange ceramic paint has been used here. It is best to apply the paint thinly when stamping on tiles already in place, to prevent it running. You can always touch it up or over-stamp if you want a denser colour.

To enhance your marine world stamping, collect flotsam and jetsam from the sea shore and use it in your room. For example, as shown in the main photograph, beached starfish can be hung from raffia strands, a collection of sea shells placed in a basket, or gather up large smooth pebbles or interestingly shaped pieces of driftwood found on walks along the beach. A good time to look is after stormy weather, when the sea has washed up all sorts of treasures onto the sands.

Jumping fish pillowcases
Plain white cotton pillowcases have been decorated with jumping fish, stamped in rows going one way and then the other way. A parchment-coloured acrylic paint, which is suitable for fabrics and is colourfast, was used.

Templates

Here is a selection of motifs all inspired by the sea. Shells make immediate and pretty images stamped around a mirror frame or on tiles, a bathroom cabinet, lampshade or cushion – the possibilities are endless. The stylised wave and fish motifs can also be used in a range of exciting and innovative ways. Look at Roman mosaics, Chinese embroideries and Japanese papercuts for inspiration. Fossils make original and unusual designs too, and here we have included a motif inspired by the wonderful spiral pattern of a fossilised ammonite.

Chapter Four

MODERN STYLE

Sharp and uncluttered lines and shapes can look very striking when applied as stamps, and the simpler the shape, the more adventurous you can be with the colours and objects that you want to stamp. If you are looking for a thoroughly modern and contemporary theme, the stamps featured in this section may be ideal for your purposes. Here, curling 'S' shapes, wavy lines, geometrics and zigzags have been stamped on ceramics, walls and fabrics.

At the beginning of the twentieth century, art and design became a lot more simplistic in its outlook. Fussy, decorative features of the Victorian period were replaced with simple and functional lines. Objects began to be designed to be primarily utilitarian and secondly decorative, rather than vice versa, as in the past.

Sourcing and adapting designs

The Art Nouveau and Art Deco movements are excellent starting points for researching stylised shapes and images. The vast amount of visuals and graphics that we see everyday in books and magazines are another obvious source of inspiration. An unusual typographic font can lead to an off-centre circle motif or an irregular, triangular border pattern, by taking the basic element of the design and using it to create your own simple stamp design.

Geometric and symmetrical patterns are very popular, although when you are stamping a surface with symmetrical designs, the motif requires a symmetry in the manner in which you apply the stamp to the surface. For example, with a geometric pattern, such as the design with one circle inside another on page 45, you can stamp at various irregular intervals, whereas with something symmetrical like the sectioned square motif shown on the curtain, the design calls for a regular pattern.

The type of material used to make stamps also gives a range of textures. The same stamping motif can be made to look very different according to the material the actual stamp is made from. If the square of irregular lines is cut from foam board or rubber the outlines will be very sharp and clear, and the colour dense and even. However, if the same stamp is cut from lino, the colour distribution will be patchy, or if it is cut from sponge, the colour will appear full of tiny holes and the outline not so sharp. With contemporary designs, as with all the other designs featured in this source book, if a particular design is something that you would like to re-use on different scales, you can reproduce the motif on a larger or smaller scale by photocopying the design and then transferring it to the stamp material. Try using one motif and at different scales and in different materials within one room for a co-ordinated effect.

Block-printed curtain

Made from a large sheet of calico, this curtain was stamped with a lino cut block of wavy lines. Using brown fabric paint, the stamp was laid one next to the other and directly beneath each other to create a constant pattern, as if screen printed as a complete image.

Folder and writing paper

A card folder in a rich blue colour was stamped with chevron tracks, cut from foam board. The stationery was stamped with a similar, but smaller stamp of a waving arrow, following the lines, set off by the chevron tracks.

Playing cards cloth

Motifs from a set of playing cards have been enlarged and cut from foam sheeting and they have then been stamped in their appropriate colours of red and black onto a cloth used for, what else, but playing cards on.

For example, take the crown and make a large stamp out of foam board and stamp it centrally onto a cushion cover. Use the same motif, cut to a much smaller scale in rubber, and stamp at various irregular points along a wall. Again, take the same motif cut out of lino on a medium scale and stamp onto plain paper, then cover notebooks with it.

An example of the crown stamp is shown here on a decorative papier mâché plate which has been painted blue and silver. The actual stamp was cut from lino because the motif has separate components to its design. If it were cut from foam or sponge the different elements would have to be cut on separate pieces, whereas with lino the design can be cut onto one piece, as the hessian backing holds it all together.

Defining modern style

The contemporary style does not class various designs as new or faddy – in fact, many designs that one would call contemporary are classic shapes that have perhaps been simplified in shape to give a sharper outline. The playing cards motifs on the table mat are emblems that date back to medieval times, yet the clean lines of the club, diamond, spade and heart create a contemporary feel, especially when stamped in the vivid and contrasting colours of red and black.

The door curtain has been stamped with a lino cut block, consisting of a square cut with wavy lines running through it. When using a lino cut, it is best to apply the paint to it with a roller as the paint is more evenly distributed than when a paintbrush is used. If you use a brush, the strokes will show up on the stamped object. However, because of the nature of lino, the paint will not transfer from the stamp onto the fabric evenly, although this patchy result, as you can see from the photograph, is actually quite effective. In this case, the lino block has been repeated in rows close to each other to give the impression of a screen-printed piece of material.

Tyre tracks inspired the chevron arrow stamped onto the stationery folder shown on page 43. You will find, as I did here, that larger stamps often do not translate when cut to smaller sizes. Thus, it is often better to take the shape of the original stamp and translate it into something slightly simpler. The chevron arrow was changed into a curling arrow

Monarch's plate

This plate is a decorative plate made from papier mâché. It was first painted white, the centre given a coat of teal blue paint and the edge painted with silver acrylic paint. The actual stamp was cut from lino, covered in silver acrylic paint and pressed firmly onto the plate, to reveal a clear crown motif.

when stamped onto the notepaper, so mimicking the original shape of the stamp but not the precise detail.

You may be inspired to stamp your walls, to highlight details on furniture or on your upholstery. The main photograph at the beginning of this chapter illustrates how the curls in the wrought iron support on the baker's stand were stamped as a border at eye level around the wall, to bring the detailing on the furniture to our notice. They have been stamped in diluted parchment-coloured emulsion paint onto a wall covered with an orange wash. This colour combination suggests the motif rather than shouting it out at you. An elongated oval with a smaller inset oval was used to decorate a utensils bag and the handles of some wooden utensils, making it an ideal gift for a keen cook.

In the template section for these contemporary designs you will notice that the motifs are either familiar or quite simple. Their simplicity and the colours you choose to work in are the factors that will make your surroundings look 'contemporary'.

Kitchen utensils and bag
A simple egg shape was cut from foam sheeting, with an off-centre egg shape cut out within it. In three varying shades it was stamped onto a utensils bag. The same motif was then reduced and cut as a stamp for the handles of the wooden kitchen utensils that were bought with the bag.

Templates

Many of these templates, although classed as contemporary, are simple geometric shapes and some are in the Art Deco style. The rising sun, sunray square, squares and stars are recognisable as Art Deco shapes, but have been simplified so that stamps can be cut easily from them.

The crown is ideal for a running theme throughout a room – stamp walls at various points throughout a room, perhaps on a softly washed grey wall, with silver acrylic paint. Then use the same stamp but cut larger as a single motif on cushions, cut smaller as a border on curtains and yet smaller still as a border to run along the lower edge of a lampshade.

The motifs like the playing cards, circles, egg, arrow and star are all adaptable for anything from stationery to fabric. Depending on the colours and the sizes used, many different effects can be achieved.

The six-pointed star looks amazing stamped in gold as a border along an orange-washed wall. As with the swirl, this can be used in different sizes; large on a wall, then tiny as a stamp on vases and ceramic plates and bowls. When stamping on glazed ceramics, they are easier to work on if they are sponged or given a light coat of paint to remove the shine and so that the stamp doesn't slip and slide so much.

Chapter Five

FRUIT & FLOWERS

*Tulips, roses, daisies, petals of all shapes
and sizes, plus a glorious array of different
leaves are all to be found in this chapter,
along with the many kinds of fruit and
vegetables, made unusual by the choice of
colours or instantly recognisable when
stamped in their own colours. These designs
are ideal if you wish to create a pretty,
country cottage style in your home.*

Gingham cushions

This stamp consists of four separate elements cut from foam sheet; a three pronged half-moon was first stamped in a purple acrylic paint, this was over-stamped twice with a wisteria-coloured half-moon. The stem was a thin strip of foam and the final step was the tiny leaf shape.

Wooden chest

This wooden box was washed with a light blue acrylic paint rubbed into the grain. Once dry, it was stamped with a yellow circle and then rounded daisy petals. One entire flower was completed before the next one was started.

Flora and fauna have inspired artists and designers as decorative elements since the beginning of time. The colours, forms, tastes and fragrances of the millions of different varieties will surely inspire us until the end of time too. An entire book could be written on such a subject and certainly all the template sections in this book could easily be dedicated to fruits and flowers.

In this section both extremely basic shapes and more intricate motifs have been used as stamps. For example, the sponged platter on page 56 is stamped with two very basic shapes which make up the speckled flower pattern. A single elongated petal shape and a single circle were cut from a dense domestic sponge. First, a circle was stamped onto the platter and then the petal shape was sponged around that circle five or six times to create a naive flower shape. Depending on the type of sponge used, the texture can be changed to add interest. In fact, if the petals were stamped with one sponge, for example a natural sponge, and the centres with a denser sponge the simplest of motifs achieves an added degree of interest. It is best to stamp the flowers individually,

Flower-stamped platter

This serving platter was stamped using sponge shapes. As with the daisy box a single circle, this time cut from a dense domestic sponge, was used with a long and pointed petal shape. The centres were stamped using a pale blue ceramic paint and the petals were done in a dark blue. The single petal shape was repeated around the circle, five or six times to produce a full flower.

rather than all the centres first, as you may find the petals overlapping and this would detract from the pattern.

The large wooden storage box was also stamped with daisies in the same manner as the platter, using two basic shapes – one single large circle and one rounded petal shape, both cut from thin foam sheeting. The box was first given a light blue stain, using water-diluted emulsion rubbed into the grain of the wood with an old rag. Once this background colour had dried, the box was stamped with canary yellow centres and huge off-white petals.

Another flower using four very simple shapes was created on the lilac gingham fabric shown on page 55. A half circle with three prongs protruding from the centre was first stamped onto the gingham in a dark purple fabric paint at various random points. A lilac quarter-moon was then stamped over these twice, turned slightly each time so that the stamped fabric looks as though it is a side view of a stylised flower. A thin strip was then stamped as the flower stem, and finally a leaf was stamped to one side of each stem.

Using fruits and vegetables

Another very simple and effective stamp was used on a plain white cotton apron using half an apple. Cut the apple in half with a smooth fruit knife (not a knife with serrated edges as this will make the apple ridged) so the apple section is as flat and as straight as possible. Remove any excess juice from the apple with a kitchen towel. Generously apply acrylic paint to the apple with a loaded paint brush and press the apple down onto the apron firmly, without moving it or rocking it from side to side. Pat the apple off on the kitchen towel until all the moisture has been removed and then re-apply the paint. You can also stamp using oranges, lemons, peppers, potatoes, and so on, as long as the excess moisture is removed before and while you stamp. Fruit and vegetable stamps do not last more than a few hours. Therefore, if you do cut a motif from one, keep an exact copy of the design so that it can be traced off onto a fresh fruit or vegetable if the previous one is no longer suitable.

Stamping on Ceramics

Ceramic objects are quite difficult to stamp and I only recommend doing so if you feel confident about your skills, especially as you will have to use ceramic paint, which requires white spirit and lots of elbow grease to remove if any mistakes are made. Three decorative plates were stamped with a stylised rose and leaves, with the rose cut from foam board and the leaves from foam sheeting because the flower was on the flat, central part of the plate and for this the foam board is suitable. However, the leaves have to fold over the ridge running around the edge

Rose-decorated plates

These decorative plates are stamped first with stylised roses and then three times with an edging of leaves in a different colour. Each plate is a different shade of pink ceramic paint. Although ceramic paint is not available in many colours, it can be mixed to the colours required. The stamp was cut from foam board, as the individual parts can then be held together by the bottom layer.

of the plate – foam sheet will bend over the plate ridge and is malleable, while foam board is not.

Try not to let the stamp slip or slide while it is face down on the plate. Ceramic paint is rather slippery, so keep a cotton bud dipped in white spirit close at hand to rectify any mistakes. Once you have removed the stamp from the plate you may find that not all of the image has transferred completely. If this happens, touch it up with a fine paint brush.

Peppers have a really interesting form, especially when simplified for a stamp. Simple white kitchen tiles were stamped alternately with red and green peppers, using ceramic paint and a lino cutting of a pepper. The effect is similar to that of stippling through a stencil, so if you do need to touch up the stamped image, do so with a fine paint brush and fill in with a stippling motion, rather than smooth brush strokes. If the tiles are going to be regularly cleaned or wiped down, then give them a couple of coats of varnish to protect them.

Kitchen tiles

Plain white ceramic tiles were given the vegetable treatment with cheerful green and red peppers. The actual stamp is made from lino and covered with ceramic paint using a lino roller to apply the paint evenly. The stamp was then placed on each tile and pressed down firmly with a heavy roller, so that the paint is evenly distributed.

Apple apron

A fresh apple was used to stamp on this thick white cotton apron. The apple was cut in half and then patted dry. Green fabric paint was applied with a brush and the apple was stamped onto the apron, flat side down, and lifted to reveal a rounded apple shape and a centre where the pips are. If you are lucky the pips may actually show up once you have stamped.

Stamping on wood

The simple wooden tray seen above, readily available in kitchen and department stores, has been brightened up with cheerful summertime daisies stamped in contrasting colours.

Before making the stamp for the tray, the slats were measured for width so that the stamp would fit neatly. The stamp was cut from foam board with only the top layer of paper and the centre layer of foam removed so that the lower layer can hold the petals together. Use a very sharp craft knife when working with foam board – if the blade is blunt, the edges of the cut foam board will become jagged and frayed. However, do ensure that the blade does not cut through the lower layer of paper, as this is the part which holds the entire stamp together.

The daisy was then stamped onto the tray in a regular pattern across the slats, all facing the same way and spaced at regular intervals. The yellow centres were painted in by hand, once all the petals were done.

Slatted tray

Before the stamp was cut for this tray, the width of the slats was measured so that the stamp would fit onto them exactly. The flower was cut from foam board, cutting through the top two layers, with the bottom layer holding the individual petals in place. This stamp was placed at regular intervals along the slats.

Templates

This section shows a selection of simple fruit, flower and leaf shapes that are easy to use as stamps and can be adapted to be either more intricate shapes or simplified even more. A variety of single leaves, petals and flower centres are shown, which can be mixed and matched with each other.

The leaves don't necessarily have to be stamped in their regular colours. Apart from their autumnal colours of reds, oranges, browns and yellows, try them in acid bright shades or in soft pastels to give them a completely different feel.

Use the different leaf shapes on one object, using the same colour, or use one stamp with lots of different colours on a single item.

You don't have to use one vegetable stamp, if you are doing a set of tiles using the same colour, stamp each tile with a different fruit or vegetable. Stamp napkins or tablecloths with the same stamps, for a co-ordinated kitchen.

Although the kitchen is the most obvious place to stamp your fruit and vegetables they look just as good in a living area. Try stamping cherries on curtains and cushions, even around a lampshade, in pinks and reds.

Chapter Six

FOLK ART

*Rustic images of animals, wildlife and
vegetation epitomise the ideas of folk art.
Foxes, hares, birds and deer roam across the
variety of stamped objects, together with
canal art motifs and simple floral patterns.
You can either choose subtle folk art shades
for your paint, or create a more
contemporary look with brighter colours.*

Folk art can be described as rustic, utilitarian and traditional, lacking in sophistication as well as having a naivety and charm which defies analysis. Folk art is the art of the people: it is found in all parts of the world and is used to decorate non-functional as well as practical objects, although in truth, folk art is mainly used for decorating everyday objects. The motifs and patterns are unique to the community from whence they sprung. Folk art in Bavaria is quite different from that in Provence, and different still from that used on the canals or by the Pennsylvanian Dutch.

Early American folk art was in essence European. Many devout religious groups who had moved to America to retain religious freedoms took with them their own styles of decoration, the best known of which is the Shaker religion with its simple heart and hand symbols which are enjoying a revival in popularity today.

Fruits are commonly used as traditional folk motifs and often have religious connotations, such as the apple from the garden of Eden or the pomegranate with its ripe red seeds being a symbol of fertility. The tulip is the most popular floral motif in folk art, particularly in Germany, England and the Low Countries during the sixteenth century. Other flowers such as roses were also especially popular, as were simple birds.

Reindeer tray

This tray was bought already distressed in a dark sky blue, with metal handles. A stylised reindeer stamp was cut from thin foam sheeting, so you can flip it around and use the back as a mirror image. Using the ribbon wrapped around the lavender as inspiration for the colour, the reindeer was stamped in dark red acrylic, To make this stamp hard wearing, coat it with polyurethane wood varnish.

Popular images are the things which surrounded the practitioners in everyday life – fruit, flowers, birds and animals.

Because much of the folk imagery which exists today is old, it will have been heavily used and thus is often worn in places or looks distressed. Stamps which may look very rustic lend themselves to this style of decoration. Folk art often gains a patina as it ages and this look may be easily contrived when stamping. In fact, whilst searching for props for this book, I came across many items which had been distressed and ready for me to stamp on.

Creating an aged look

A good way to create a distressed background on varnished wood is to remove the varnish using coarse sandpaper. Then use a finer sandpaper to smooth the piece. Using a primer, paint a white or light-coloured base colour onto the object and leave to dry. Paint a second colour, leave this to dry, and then repeat with a third colour and allow this to dry. Sand away the top coat to reveal some of the second and base coat colours. The colours may be different shades of the same colour or in complete contrast. You can add an aged sheen by rubbing in a tinted furniture polish.

To age an item you can create a craquleur. This is done by applying two coats of varnish on top of one another which have different drying times and do not like one another. Apply the second varnish while the first coat is still wet. The result is a crazing in the varnish which may be enhanced by rubbing burnt umber oil paint into the cracks.

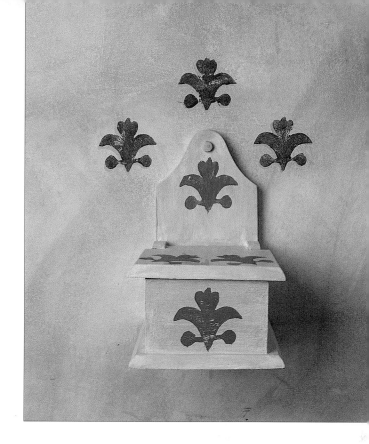

Salt box
A wooden salt box has been painted with cream emulsion, layered with yellow paint and then distressed with sandpaper to reveal the cream. A canal art inspired motif of a bud and two balls has then been stamped onto it.

Wall hooks
This plain set of wall hooks was washed in three different shades of light blue, to achieve an aged look. Then the fox and the hare were stamped on in a rust colour. When dry, they were over-stamped and staggered with parchment paint, creating a shadow effect.

67

A small cupboard, bird house and coat hooks were all distressed using different shades of blue. The cupboard has been stamped using a leaf shape in light green, with a small tulip stamped in pink. The pretty colours used and the small scale make this suitable for a cottage setting. The bird house was already distressed when bought and the most obvious motif to use was a bird. The stamp was cut from foam sheet and different shades of blues were applied so that the bird changes colour.

The coat hooks were painted with two different blues and then sanded to give an uneven colour. A hare being chased by a fox was stamped above the hooks first in rust and then over-stamped in parchment. The over-stamping is a little to one side of the original stamp causing a shadow effect and giving a feeling of speed and movement.

A simple wooden stool was first sanded to remove the varnish and then painted with acrylic in an off-white shade. A random leaf pattern was stamped in terracotta to give a folk-art effect. A jug was given a coat of emulsion to provide a matt surface and the same leaf pattern applied.

Modern folk images

Folk art does not have to be crude – it can be simple with a home-spun look as shown in the stamped cushions. The warm colours of burnt orange and pink-tinged terracotta were picked from a hand-woven throw made from silk linen and wool. The cushion covers were made with a chequerboard pattern created by tiny seams sewn up, down and across the fabric. An unusual flower pattern stamp was created from a very simple shape which was turned ninety degrees each time it was stamped.

A blue slatted tray was stamped using a very striking plum colour paint and a folk style deer motif. Decoration need not be overpowering or with many repeats, as this tray shows. Remember, a simple pattern often works well so do not be tempted to add too much detail.

A salt box was one common household item often decorated in a folk art style. The one shown on page 67 uses a traditional canal art symbol updated with contemporary colours. The Scandinavian colours of yellow and blue have a clean cool appearance.

As shown in this chapter's photographs, folk art may be old in appearance, warm and stylish as in the throw and cushions, or very modern as in the salt box. It all depends on the look you want to achieve for your home.

Patchwork-style cushions

The fabric used here is a light linen sewn with a crossways tuck to produce patchwork-like squares. These squares have then been used as a guide to stamp petal shapes into their corners; the stamp is turned 90 degrees each time it is stamped in an adjacent square, to create a flower pattern.

Harvest jug and stool

This creamy coloured ceramic jug had a shiny glaze, so it was first sponged with emulsion and then stamped with the hollow leaf shape. This jug is used purely for decorative purposes as the paint is not waterproof. If you need to make it waterproof, use ceramic paints and then bake it according to the instructions to make it safe.

Templates

Naive and rustic images are used in folk art and are often made to look older than they actually are. Many of these stamp templates are of simple leaf shapes, done in a very simple, almost childlike way. Good examples of this are the hollow leaf stamped on the jug and stool and the floating leaf stamped in a light green colour on the decorative cupboard, together with the simple pink tulip head.

Many animals are featured here as these are also popular folk art images. Simplified birds, like the bird stamped on the bird house cupboard, defy their simple outlines in the way you can stamp the colours.

On the bird house, the bird stamp had the paint applied to it with a flat paint brush, using a light blue paint graduating into a darker blue as the tail feathers. One of the advantages of applying paint to a stamp with a brush is the paint effects you can achieve with the brush which then transfer onto the object that you are stamping. You can also make speckles, zigzags, squares – in fact any patterns on the surface of the stamp which would then transfer onto the stamped object.

Chapter Seven

ROMANTIC MOODS

Pink hearts and budding flowers, rosy cupids and winding bows, old lace and doves in flight all encapsulate the spirit of the romantic. Although there is a variety of stamps in the motif section, the main image is the heart in its many forms.

The heart is a centuries' old symbol of love and friendship. It occurs in many different cultures and is one of the most universal tokens of affection. As a motif for stamping in the home, it can be used in many ways and in many different forms.

Hearts in all manner of shapes, sizes, styles and forms are to be found over the next few pages, plus a scattering of other romantic motifs, such as cupids, bows, ribbons and doves. Do not restrict yourself to using only shades of red and pink for these images. You can always experiment with bright and unexpected colours for a more contemporary look, or with subtle and faded hues for a softer traditional feel.

Window style

In the main photograph on page 74, simple hearts in various shapes and sizes have been stamped onto a pelmet, curtain and window border in a feminine pearlescent pink paint. The MDF pelmet was first painted with two coats of white emulsion, sanded with a fine grade sandpaper and then given a final coat of emulsion for a smooth and even finish. The triangular border pattern was measured before the heart stamp was cut, so that the heart fitted perfectly into each triangle.

The floaty voile curtain made an ideal surface to stamp on in a regular pattern as the checks can be used as a guide. However, when stamping on such fine fabric, take care and lay newspaper beneath the fabric while stamping to avoid the paint seeping right through onto the work surface. Also ensure that there is not too much paint on the stamp when working on this type of fabric as it does tend to smudge if there is excess paint.

Once the curtain and pelmet were in position, the border below the window was added as a finishing touch, using a different shaped heart, but in the same pearly pink colour. Although this was done as a border, you could stamp hearts all around the room at irregular and spaced out points. This kind of look would be perfect in a young girl's room, as all little girls seem to love soft pink and hearts.

A completely different style has been achieved in a kitchen setting by stamping yet another curtain with a small heart. Gingham is a great fabric to stamp on, as the cotton is ideal for accepting paint well and the checks guide your pattern.

Gingham curtain

A simple heart has been cut from foam sheet to fit the squares of the large red and white gingham fabric. Using the squares of the gingham as a guide, the red hearts have been stamped in every other white square.

Shaker images

The Shaker image of the heart and hand illustrates their motto of 'Hands to work, hearts to God'. A lino cut was made from the template of the heart-in-hand motif. The best way to copy a design onto lino is to trace it onto the lino using carbon paper. It is important to remember that the areas where you remove lino will not stamp and it is only the lino that remains in relief that will stamp colour onto your surface.

Bucket and plate

This Shaker-type motif has been stamped onto a galvanised bucket and plain white china plate. These are very simple and Shaker-like in appearance, as is the dark blue colour and the traditional lino cut stamp motif.

The Shaker theme is reflected in the objects stamped – the galvanised metal bucket, used here as a flower pot, and a plain white china plate. When stamping china, the china must be for decorative use only, especially if you are not using ceramic paints. Most ceramic paints are still not ideal to eat off, as the more you wash them, the more likely it is that the colour will come off the plate and onto the food.

Hearts and cupids

The small wall cupboard was painted a candy floss pink and then stamped on with white paint. The romantic images are again hearts, but this time they are accompanied by cupids holding out hearts as gifts. Because the heart motif is such a simple and popular motif you can't really go wrong with it. The theme is continued with a cloudy, sky blue wall behind, turning the cupboard into a special storage place for your treasured items.

Doves are renowned as the traditional messengers of love and if a romantic window blind is what you want (see page 81), this dove stamp

Miniature trug

A beautiful gift to give is this tiny wooden trug, which has been painted a dark purple and then stamped with light blue ribbon shapes. It has been filled with a selection of purple, lavender and lilac summer flowers.

Corner cupboard

An MDF corner cupboard has been given a candy floss pink make-over and covered in hearts and cupids, to make it an ideal display unit for any soft-hearted romantic. This type of design is particularly liked by girls of all ages.

False book

This wonderful false book, suitable for storing love letters and old photographs, was painted with a rich pearlescent lavender colour. Several coats had to be applied above a white primed base for the colour to look right. A winged heart was stamped in the centre of the book.

is perfect. Take a light coloured fabric blind, in this case it is yellow, as the light from the window will pass through it and give it a warm glow. Sponge on white and blue paint to give it a cloudy background effect. If you cut the stamp out of thin foam sheet, it can be reversed so that the doves are flying in all directions. Because the blind is made from a synthetic fabric, the paint does not lie evenly, but the dappled effect created is interesting.

A lovely home-made gift to give as a token of friendship and love is this very romantic miniature trug, full to overflowing with dried lavender and fresh forget-me-nots. This trug was bought in plain MDF in its original brown colour. The first thing to do is to sand and then prime the base with white emulsion paint, so that you have a light colour to begin with. A strong purple was chosen as the base colour, applied in three coats to give an even finish. Two bows with long trails were cut to fit along the long and short sides of the trug. They were stamped in a sharply contrasting light blue. These colours are quite unusual, yet have a striking effect and show how you do not have to stick to the traditional

Dove blind

A light coloured blind was sponged with blue and white paint for a cloudy effect, then romantic doves were stamped on. When the sun shines through a lovely dappled glow shows.

Heart-shaped boxes

Five heart-shaped boxes that live in a larger round box were given a coat of white paint and stamped with a lacy heart inspired by a tablecloth design. The box is lined with lace to offset the stamp design.

Square wooden box

A plain square box was painted white and stamped with a red intricate heart within a heart lino cut. Due to the nature of lino, the paint is patchy, giving the box an aged look.

romantic colours of white, pink and red. Always try to experiment with colours before you even begin to stamp on surfaces, as you will find that some of the most unlikely combinations of colours can give the most wonderful results.

A lacy heart lino cut was used to a different effect on a plain white painted box. The stamp was cut precisely to fit the lids of the smaller boxes which sit snugly inside the large, round box. Lino cuts give massively varying results depending on the surface that you stamp. On ceramics and metal, as with the hand-and-heart motif on page 77, they appear quite smooth and even; however, on some surfaces, such as fabric and wood, the finished result is often uneven and patchy. This kind of result resembles an aged look, but if it is not to your taste, it can be rectified by using a lino roller, which is a heavy rubber roller, to apply an even pressure to the back of the lino stamp as it is laid on the surface you are decorating. Alternatively, you can touch up the detail with a fine paint brush after removing the stamp.

Templates

*Everybody loves hearts – they show
affection and warmth when given to
someone as a gift, whether it be a heart
on some note paper or a gift wrapped in
heart-stamped wrapping paper.*

*Many of the templates are variations
on the simple heart in different styles,
there's a lacy heart, a winged heart, a
heart in a stripy circle and a heart with
a triangular border.*

*If you don't like the sweet effects of
the pink and red hearts, stamp in vivid
and acid colours, like lime green and
electric blue rather than sticking to the
more usual colours.*

*Roses are romantic flowers so several
different roses have been included, such
as a stylised rose and a simple rose
outline. Also, two variations on a bow
have been featured. These can be
stamped alone, as with the miniature
trug, or arranged together with some
hearts and flowers.*

*The dove is a bird that symbolises
peace to all cultures. It looks great on
the blind, but you can go large scale
with it, by washing a wall with blue
and white paint to make it look cloudy
and then stamp birds all over it.*

Chapter Eight

THE ETHNIC LOOK

Ethnic is a word that encapsulates many different things – what is seen as ethnic in America is very different to what is perceived as ethnic in Europe or in Asia. In the Western world, ethnic is a word that describes the beautiful, hand-made objects from exotic places – kelims from Morocco, wood carvings from India, turquoise jewellery from Mexico, Navajo motifs, paisley flowers taken from rich textiles, and cats' eyes inspired by Ancient Egypt.

Many of the templates for stamps featured in this section have in fact been inspired by objets d'art from all around the world, including motifs picked from Navajo rugs, Indian textiles, stylised exotic animals from around the globe and North African carvings.

Shapes that are not considered 'ethnic' can be adapted by using colours that are deemed exotic, unusual and vivid. So simple shapes like a jagged semi-circle and a squared-off flower, although not 'ethnic' shapes, can be used with certain colours to make them appear as such.

The unusual cat's eye block was inspired by a museum display of old wooden printing blocks for textiles. The stamp was made from a 12 cm (5 in) square of foam sheet with triangular shapes cut out. Opposing rows of triangles produce the cat's eye effect. The stamp has been saturated in a dark blue paint and then stamped onto an orange cotton fabric. Press down on the stamp firmly, perhaps even running a dry roller over it so that the paint is distributed evenly on the fabric. This kind of stamp block can be made using many different motifs as a repetitious block. Use straightforward and simple shapes, like circles, diamonds and lines, so as not to over-complicate the design. Experiment and see whether you want to stamp these blocks one next to the other so that the whole fabric is covered, like the cushion cover shown here, or whether you prefer the occasional block here and there.

A huge fabric lampshade was given the 'ethnic' treatment by stamping proud peacocks around the lower edge of the lampshade. Because the weave of

Cat's eye cushion

This cushion was made up with an orange linen fabric that has been stamped with a cat's eye block, cut from foam sheeting. The block was stamped so that each stamp was very close to each other and directly below each other; it looks as though it could have been screen printed, but was actually done with the block, which is a 12 cm (5 in) square.

the fabric is so heavy, when the peacocks were stamped onto it, the colour did not transfer in a solid manner, in fact, coverage was quite patchy. However, the outline was very clear, so places where the coverage was not too even were touched up with a fine paint brush loaded with paint. When touching up a heavy fabric, apply the paint in a stippling manner, to allow the paint to fill in all the awkward sections.

A paisley-shaped flower, inspired by many Indian textiles, was cut from foam sheet and stamped along the inside rim of the blue glazed bowl shown on page 90. If you want to stamp a bowl like this for purely decorative purposes, you can use ceramic or acrylic paint and then varnish over it with polyurethane varnish or even PVA. Stamping on ceramics is difficult because of the slippery and rounded surfaces and if you use ceramic paint it can add to the difficulty. As the bowl will be for decorative purposes only, I recommend that you stamp it in acrylic and then varnish.

Beneath the paisley flower bowl is a snake-stamped table mat. A snake is perhaps one of the easiest kinds of stamps to make – the form can be long and winding or fat and curling. Here the snake was stamped onto orange material in a slightly paler orange shade of paint. The fabric has quite a loose weave so the texture achieved with the stamp looks suitably faded and old.

American Indian motifs

A single motif of a diamond shape with lines protruding from the outside edge and a block set in the middle was taken from an American Indian rug. This image was cut out of foam board, which is the easiest material to work with as the block in the centre can be held in place by

Peacock lampshade
A plain off-white fabric lampshade has been stamped with large peacocks walking around its lower edge, alternating their colours between orange and dark blue. The grain on the fabric was extremely knobbly making the stamping quite difficult, so the outline was actually filled in with a paint brush to make the colour heavier.

Miniature chest of drawers

A tiny chest of drawers suitable for trinkets has been given a light blue wash with diluted acrylic worked into the surface and then rubbed into the grain with an old rag. Once dry, a motif taken from a Navajo blanket was cut from foam board, then stamped onto each drawer front in Prussian blue.

Captain's chair

A motif was taken from the same Navajo blanket, but a different five diamond shape. This was enlarged and carefully measured as it is a symmetrical shape and could very easily look off-centre. This was stamped using acrylic paint suitable for fabrics onto the chair back in a row of three and on the seat in a pattern of five.

Paisley bowl and cloth

This decorative blue glazed bowl has been stamped with a dark orange acrylic paint along the inside edge with a simple paisley flower motif taken from Indian textile work. The cloth was stamped with the same paint.

the lower layer of paper. This motif was then stamped onto a dark terracotta cotton fabric, with yellow and Prussian blue acrylic paint. Choose acrylic paints which are suitable for fabrics. Read the instructions on the paint packaging, as some acrylic paints are colourfast, once they have been ironed on the reverse. The fabric was then made up into a striking cushion cover.

The same motif was also stamped onto a small chest of drawers, which was washed with water-diluted sky blue emulsion paint. The grain was highlighted by rubbing the paint in with an old rag. Once the wash had dried, a single stamp was placed on each drawer using a contrasting darker blue paint.

Another complementary motif used here is the five adjoining diamonds. This traditional motif was an element of a design also taken from the American Indian rug, which you can see photographed with the captain's chair. The chair was stamped with the five diamonds used in an enlarged form. You can enlarge or reduce any of the templates by using the sizing facility on a photocopier or by scaling up or down on graph paper. Here, the five diamonds motif has been stamped in a regular pattern across the chair's fabric back and seat with a maroon acrylic paint. The back of the fabric was then ironed to make it colourfast.

The templates here are only to inspire or catalyse your own thoughts. There is a wealth of visual sources around you to pick and choose from. Motifs of an 'ethnic' kind can be picked up from so many places, from prints and weaves in textiles to architectural fittings.

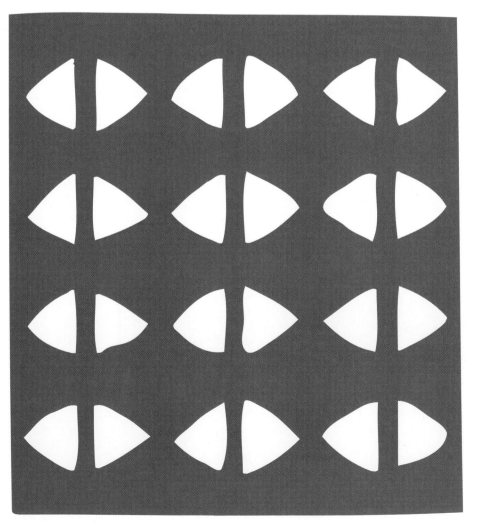

Templates

These are what one could call the more exotic motifs in the book, inspired by beautiful objects from many cultures.

Motifs have been chosen from various textiles from around the world. For example, the two Navajo emblems were taken from a blanket which you can see beside the captain's chair. If you single out certain elements of a design from something like a rug or blanket, you can relate the surrounding objects to that to tie a whole room's decor together.

Lucky charm motifs are also featured with the scarab beetle. This can be stamped in shimmering colours on note paper, gift wrapping and boxes to wish the recipients good luck.

The cat's eye block, inspired by a visit to an art gallery and a series of old wooden printing blocks, is unusual in that it is the areas that are not stamped that reveal the image.

Other images like the jagged semi-circle border pattern and the square flower shape come to life depending on the brightness of the colours you stamp with. To achieve an 'ethnic' look, choose vivid colours – oranges, bright greens, reds and yellows. However, don't overload your space with too many colours. If you are stamping a room to the 'ethnic' theme, tie in the colours of the surroundings with the stamp colours. For example, if your sofa has a little red and blue in the pattern, pick up on it and bring it out with some bold red hausa-shaped stamps as a border along the wall, then add some blue details here and there.

In a room, try to keep the different colours to a minimum, just two or three colours should be used to carry on a theme, otherwise it can look messy.

93

Chapter Nine

CHILDREN'S STAMPING

Stamping is a quick and simple way of transforming a plain adult environment into a cheerful, childlike one. Children love bright colours and bold shapes, so the combination of colourful backgrounds and simple shapes stamped onto them appeal to youngsters of all ages.

This chapter includes simple animal outlines of dogs, cats, crocodiles, lizards and ducks, as well as a story-time smiling moon, teddy bear and mushroom.

A bedroom or playroom wall painted in plain colours may be embellished with a stamped decoration using a variety of different colours. They can be bright eye-catching reds, purples, yellows, blues and greens or the more subtle ice cream and pistachio shades. Walls need not be the only surfaces to receive this treatment. All kinds of furniture, especially old or tired-looking pieces, may be cleaned, primed and then painted and stamped with a new, fun design.

As you will see from the children's templates, the outlines given are very simple in shape, designed especially to appeal to children of a very young age. Because they are so simple, they are probably the easiest to make and stamp, so perhaps this section is the best one to start off with if you are a beginner. Your children may also like to join in the fun and help to decorate their own rooms with stamps that echo their hobbies and interests.

From the many templates of animals in the template section, ducks were chosen to stamp onto a little orange chair. Because the stamp was cut from thin foam sheeting, you can flip the stamp over so that the image is reversible. This means that the ducks on the chair back face each other. Stamp one duck, clean the foam, apply paint on the other side and then stamp the image so it is facing the opposite way to the previous one.

Children's storage

Children need storage for all their belongings in the same way that adults do. Shoe boxes are ideal for all manner of small items, from toys, jigsaws and games, especially those with lots of tiny pieces to lose, to child-sized items of clothing such as gloves and socks. A preparatory coat of white emulsion paint will obliterate any writing on the boxes. More than one coat may be required before the print disappears and the box is ready to be painted with a bright colour and stamped. If you are decorating boxes for younger children, the brighter the colours the better. These boxes shown here were painted with fuchsia pink and canary yellow emulsion. It is best to paint about three coats, allowing each coat to dry properly before starting the next, as this will give you a smooth and even finish.

All children love animals and many of the stamps in this chapter are simple animal shapes. Here, leaping cats and smiling crocodiles are

Duck chair
A tiny child's chair has been painted with a rich orange emulsion. The seat and chair back have yellow swimming ducks stamped along the seat in rows of three, with two facing each other on the back of the chair. To keep the image from wear and tear, varnish the chair with a colourless polyurethane varnish.

stamped on the boxes. They do not have to be stamped in a regular pattern – you can go for a single large stamp, evenly spaced smaller stamps or spontaneous, irregular stamps dotted around the boxes. Shoe boxes are great to practise on as most people have them around the house.

Another much larger storage box stamped in this chapter is a collapsible fabric toy box. This is made in a strong turquoise blue and the stamps needed to be in keeping with the brightness. So vivid pink, orange, lime green and yellow were chosen to complement the base colour. We used acrylic paints to stamp on this box as fabric paints tend to soak into heavier cotton fabric, absorb the background colour and lose their original brightness. Most acrylic paints are colourfast on fabrics, but do check that the paint you use is suitable before you begin.

The stamp used to make these large dots was the sponge lid of a pin box, but you could use a dense sponge just cut into a circle – what could be simpler? The bright colours were then stamped randomly all over the box sides and lid. You may find that the edges of the circle will not be

Fabric toy box
A large collapsible fabric box has been stamped with fun spots. The stamp was just a circle of sponge saturated in brightly coloured acrylic paints. Because the fabric is quite heavy, fabric paint would soak through the material leaving a dull colour behind, whereas with acrylic paint the colour lies on top of the fabric.

Shoe boxes

Children's shoe boxes have been painted with bright acrylic paints and then stamped with leaping cats and smiling crocodiles in sharply contrasting colours.

sharp. If you do not like this, just use a paint brush to fill in the edges with a smooth brush stroke.

Bags are yet another good surface to decorate. Bags are used for all occasions including swimming, picnics and carrying school books. A child's duffel bag on page 103 has been given the stamping treatment with randomly placed blue stamps of a smiling moon. Children love simple shapes and bright colours, especially things that remind them of stories that they have heard. So characters from fairy stories could be translated into simple shapes and made into stamps, once you are confident of your skills in making stamps.

Everyone needs places to hang their clothes and even plain hooks can be stamped with children in mind. An MDF hook was primed with white emulsion and then painted with several layers of tangerine orange paint. The Scottie dog stamp was cut from thin foam sheeting, which is ideal for small curved shapes as it is easy to cut with a sharp craft knife. As with the duck chair, the dog has been stamped on one side of the centre hook and then the stamp has been flipped over and used on the other side of the centre hook, facing the first dog. The clothes hanger was stamped with a bone motif to complement the hook. Quirky ideas like this can be used with many motifs, for example, cats and fish, hens and eggs, fox and hare (as seen in the Folk Art chapter).

Friezes and furniture

The frieze overleaf features another of the animals in the template section. This particular lizard stamp is ideal for little boys who like amphibians and crawling animals. The frieze is made from a wide strip of wall lining paper that has been given a cloudy yellow wash. An entire wall can be lined with such paper and then stamped, making an inexpensive and individual alternative to conventional wallpaper. Here, glittery blue paint has been used to give a metallic finish to the lizards.

Outdoor furniture can be stamped, although if it is going to be left outside, it will need to be varnished to protect the paint from the elements. A child's picnic bench was stamped with bright gardening tools.

Hook and hanger

An MDF wall hanger was primed in white emulsion before being given three coats of tangerine emulsion paint. A Scottie dog motif was cut from foam sheet, stamped on one side of the centre hook, facing inwards, then flipped over and stamped on the other side. Varnish the hook to protect the stamped image. Hangers were stamped with bones, to complement the hooks.

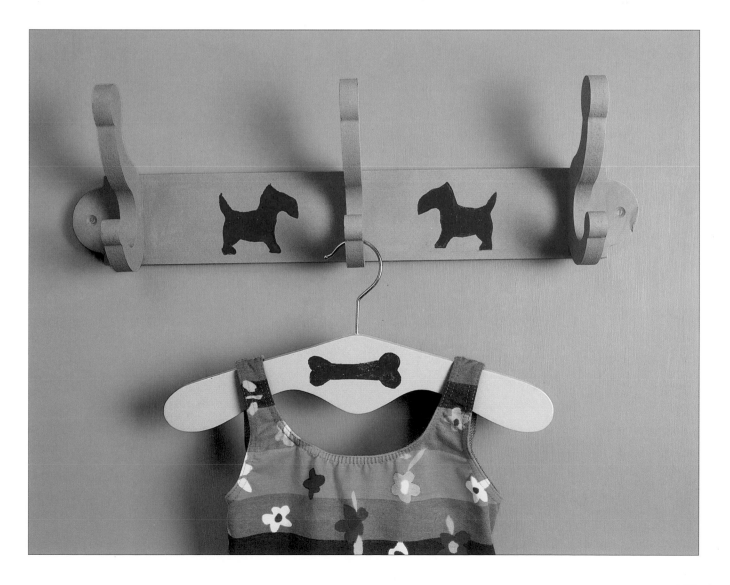

This stamp is unusual as the same stamp is used for the handles of both tools, while the tool part of the fork and trowel are interchanged, so that it looks as if each tool has been stamped individually. The handles were stamped first and then the trowels and forks were stamped alternately.

With a child's room one can get away with using lots of colours and different stamps. This is probably the one room in the house that can never look too busy or too bright, as children of all ages need constant visual stimulation.

Alternatively, keep a wall white and let the children do their own stamping using water-based paints. When you get tired of the wall, simply paint it over with white emulsion and start all over again.

Wall frieze

Lining paper has been cut in half lengthways and given an orange wash with diluted acrylic paint. The lizard stamps were done in a dark glittery blue paint, so that in a certain light the lizards shimmer with a metallic edge.

Picnic bench

A child's picnic bench was edged with gardening tools. The handles were stamped first, so that the top edges reached the metal screws in the bench. These were incorporated into the stamped design as holding the handles and the tools together.

Duffel bag

A child's cotton duffel bag has been covered with smiling moons. The stamp was cut from foam sheet and covered with acrylic paint, which is suitable for fabrics and colourfast, once it has been ironed on the reverse.

Templates

The templates for the children's stamps are very simple outlines of images that all children love, with animals featuring in particular.

The Scottie dog as seen on the hooks is great. Once you are a little more experienced in stamping, you may want to try some paint effects in your stamping. Using a fine paint brush and different coloured paints, paint a tartan pattern onto the stamp. This has to be done quite quickly before the paint dries, and then stamp onto a surface to reveal a tartan Scottie dog stamp. Use the bone and paw prints to accompany the dog.

Other animals include the butterfly in flight, the smiling friendly crocodile and the leaping cat. When stamping for children, the best way to go about it is to choose your child's favourite colours and splash the colour on.

There are stamps for the child who likes planes, gardening and teddy bears. Because they are so simple, many of these stamps are suitable to be cut from sponge and stamped around large surfaces like walls and floors.

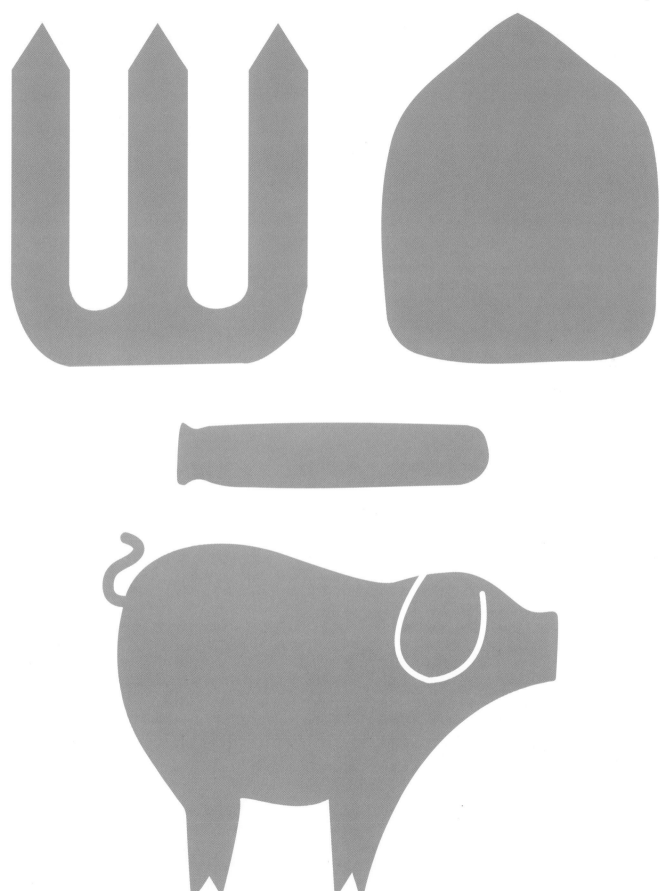

A B C

G H I J

N O P

U V W

D E F

K L M

Q R S T

X Y Z

Chapter Ten

PARTY
TIME

Occasions worth celebrating are ideal
opportunities to test your stamping skills.
Gift wrapping, cards, decorative table
settings and invitations are suitable for all
types of festivities from Christmas and
Thanksgiving to Easter and Halloween.
These are times of the year when one can
really go over the top to create that special
festive mood with stamping.

Gift wrap

*Plain brown and green packaging paper
have been transformed into festive gift
wrap with a stylised Christmas tree cut
from lino, and a lyre cut from foam
board. Because the strings on the lyre
are too fine to cut as a stamp they were
drawn in later with a white pencil.
Plain tissue has also been stamped with
tiny shimmering motifs.*

Festive blind

*This luscious blind is suitable for any
special occasion with its stars and suns
glowing warmly on the red background.
The stamps were cut from foam
sheeting, then stamped using gold
acrylic paint. When candle light or a
soft glow from a lamp catch the sun
and stars they twinkle.*

Everybody decorates their home at Christmas, from hanging decorations on the tree to dressing up the dining room table. What better way to do this than making your own stamps and then transforming your home with them. You can stamp a whole range of dining wear to create a themed dinner service. Try stamping a tablecloth, napkins, place mats and cards either with a constant motif in different sizes and same colours or with various motifs that tie in with each other.

A neat and modern idea for a crisp white linen tablecloth is to stamp it with a stylised Christmas tree spaced at even intervals around the edge of the cloth, creating a border. This same stamp can be used on white napkins, placed in one corner as a single motif. Continue the theme and place the stamp centrally on a side plate or serving platter. Cut a smaller stamp as a simple Christmas tree silhouette and using silver acrylic paint, stamp onto hand-made paper. Cut the paper into little name cards for the dinner table.

Create gift wrapping for the presents that you give to your loved ones on special occasions. The plainest brown packaging paper can be transformed into stylish gift wrap by stamping in luxurious colours. Here, brown paper has been stamped with silver lyres, the strings drawn on afterwards with white pencil crayon. Other inexpensive wrappings like

tissue paper can be stamped – here, white tissue was stamped with a silvery white paint, just giving a hint of sparkle to the package.

When the weather is cold, the nights are dark and Christmas is just around the corner, it is great to close the curtains early and make yourself comfortable and cosy in your home, while nature takes its course outside. To complement your room decorations, keep the curtains tied back and pull down a specially decorated festive blind. The stamps on the red blind were cut from foam sheet and then stamped at various points with gold acrylic paint.

Make your own Christmas stockings by cutting two wide sock shapes out of velvet or silk offcuts. Sew them together with the right sides facing and then turn them around the right way. Stamp a row of green packages along a wide strip of white satin, using a lino cut with dark green fabric paint.

Greetings cards

*Hand-made paper has been stamped
with simple festive logos of stars and a
bird before it was cut out. The paper
was then measured, the fold marked off,
then half the top outline was cut
around using a sharp craft knife. When
the card is then folded along the
marked edge, the motif stands up
smartly to attention.*

Stamp steadily as the stamp can be prone to slipping on the satin. Sew
the cuff onto the top open edge of the stocking and add a ribbon for
hanging. You can adjust the size of the stocking according to the size of
the presents you hope to receive!

Even a picture frame can be given a festive touch. A plain square,
wooden picture frame has been given the Christmas treatment by painting it with silver acrylic paint. This acrylic paint looks amazing after
three or four coats, transforming the frame to make it look like chrome.
It has then been stamped with a very simple green holly motif and makes
a perfect present.

Make your own greeting cards by stamping onto hand-made paper.
Stamp the image before you cut out the card shape and then measure

around the stamp to get the measurements right. A novel idea is to make the stamp stand up in relief. Do this by cutting around the top half of the image with a craft knife before folding the card in half. When the card is folded, the image will pop up and stand out. This technique can be used with all manner of greeting cards; the only restriction is that you should use card or a very heavy paper, otherwise the card will buckle and tend to fall over.

For a Halloween or Thanksgiving party, why not decorate your own stationery with black cats or crossed broomsticks, especially if you are sending out party invitations. As these are ideal themes for parties, overleaf I have created a fun children's tea table, complete with a decorated tablecloth and napkins. The matching orange placemats are made from a sheet of thin card and stamped with a single triangle to form the eyes, nose and mouth.

Easter table

Easter is a time of regeneration, so stamping motifs can mimic the signs of Spring – use egg shapes, chicks, bunnies, Easter bonnets. If you are decorating a table for Easter, reflect the mood with the colours you use – lots of pastel colours, spring-like yellows and blues, shades of lavender and soft pinks. Use an Easter chick motif around the tablecloth, interspersed with complete or cracked eggs, symbolising rebirth. The eggs

Holly picture frame
A square wooden picture frame has been painted with four coats of silver acrylic on top of a white primed base, making the frame look as though it is made from chrome. It was then stamped with a simple pair of holly leaves that are attached to each other by their stalks.

117

Halloween tea party

*A children's Halloween tea party
includes stamped accessories to get them
in the mood. The paper tablecloth was
stamped with a border of crossed
broomsticks and cat silhouettes, with
matching black cat paper napkins.*

Easter tablecloth and plate

*A white tablecloth has been decorated
for a children's Easter lunch with yellow
chicks and blue eggs running along the
border. The white plate has been
stamped to match the tablecloth, with a
blue chick in the centre and tiny yellow
daisies around the edge.*

stamped on the cloth shown here were treated to some speckles using a
nearly dry paint brush dipped in parchment-coloured paint. If you do
not want to stamp on your best white linen, buy a good quality paper
cloth – the results will be just as good. Stamp Easter bonnets on the place
cards and ribbons on the napkins.

Other occasions like St Valentine's Day, Mother's Day, christenings
and weddings all require some kind of festivity. One simple motif can be
carried on throughout a dinner setting for each of these occasions –
hearts for St Valentine's Day, roses for Mother's Day, crosses for a christening and bells for a wedding. These motifs can be in various sizes, but
keep them simple and stick to one or at the most two colours, otherwise
it can look a little over the top.

For Valentine's Day, a betrothal, anniversary or christening celebra-
tion, use the dove or borrow a heart or bows from the Romantic Moods
chapter of the book. A trumpet can be used to fanfare congratulations
on passing an important exam or test.

Templates

I have tried to include many different types of special occasions in this chapter's templates and many are suitable for more than one particular occasion.

For weddings, the horseshoe, cupid, lyre and trumpet, ribbons and bells are all suitable, especially when stamped in the right colours. Stamp white table cloths, napkins and place cards with the silver musical instruments and ribbon borders. For occasions like Mother's Day and Valentine's Day you will find other suitable templates in the romantic and flowers chapters.

Stamps like suns, stars or moons are suitable for all celebrations. They can be stamped in pearlescent colours to lift them out of the background and look especially good on a dark background.

The snowflake motif is good for Thanksgiving, depending on the weather you have at that time of year. It can also be used for birthdays that are celebrated in winter time and, of course, for Christmas.

All these stamps are quite festive, but a lot of the effect comes from the colour of the background you stamp on and the colour of the stamps.

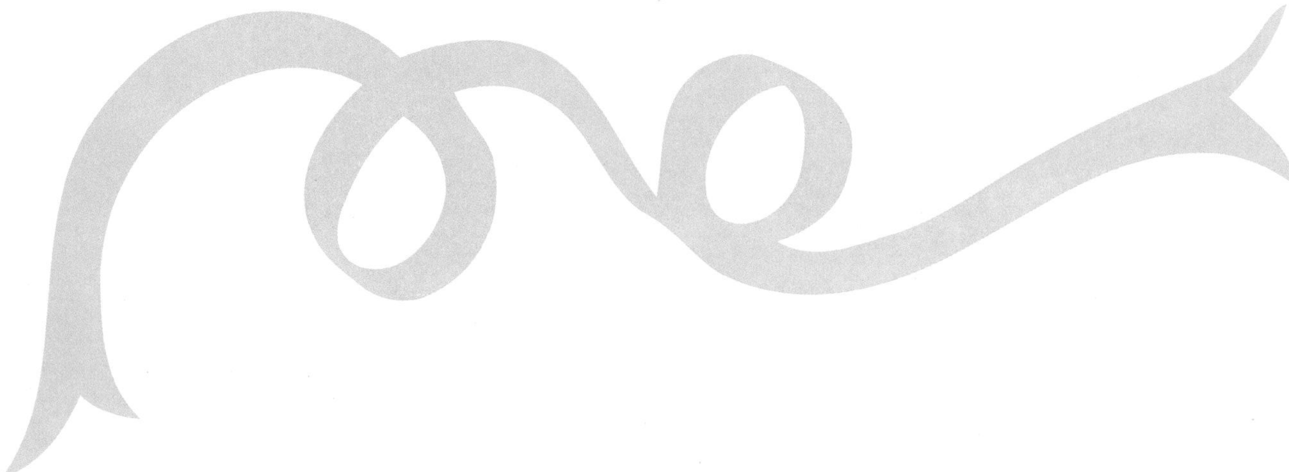

Suppliers

Many thanks to the following manufacturers who were so generous with their help in putting this book together.

Daler Rowney Ltd
Doncaster Road
Southern Industrial Area
Bracknell
Berks RG12 8ST
Tel 01344 424621
(*paints*)

Fred Aldous
PO Box 135
37 Lever Street
Manchester M60 1UX
Tel 0161 236 2477
Fax 0161 236 6075
(*craft supplies*)

Jali Lifestyle
Apsley House
Chartham
Canterbury
Kent CT4 7HT
Tel 01227 831710
Fax 01277 831950
(*decorative woodwork*)

Liquitex
Binney and Smith Europe Ltd
Ampthill Road
Bedford MK42 9RS
Tel 01234 360201
Fax 01234 342110
(*paints*)

MFI
Southon House
333 The Hyde
Edgware Road
Colindale
London NW9 6TD
Tel 0181 205 8823
(*furniture and bedding*)

Offray
Fir Tree Place
Church Road
Ashford
Middlesex TW15 2PH
Tel 01784 247281
Fax 01784 248597
(*ribbons*)

Pebeo
North Way
Andover
Hampshire SP10 5BE
Tel 01264 33171
(*ceramic paints*)

Prices
110 York Road
London SW11 3RU
Tel 0171 228 3345
Fax 0171 738 0197
(*candles*)

The Pier/Pier One USA
153 Milton Park
Abingdon
Oxfordshire OX14 4SD
Tel 01235 821088
Fax 01235 821011
(*decorative accessories*)

Woodspirits UK
Unit 42
New Lyndenburg Estate
New Lyndenburg Street
London SE7 8NF
Tel/Fax 0181 293 4949
(*soaps*)

Author's Acknowledgements

I should like to thank everyone who helped to make this book, including my invaluable assistant Labeena, Shona the photographer, Gillian the editor, and Cindy for commissioning me and having faith in us to make the book what it is.

Index